BURIED ALIVE

A corrupt judicial system, fake friends, deceit, the trial…This is Davon's story coming from the streets of Baltimore City.

DAVON ROBERTS

PAGE PUBLISHING
Conneaut Lake, PA

First originally published by Page Publishing 2022

ISBN 979-8-88654-688-0 (pbk)
ISBN 979-8-88654-691-0 (digital)

Printed in the United States of America

This book is dedicated to my

Aunt Delores Jones (Dee-Dee)
Father Melvin Lee Bomar Jr. (Dad)
Grandmother Louise "Dixie" Brown (Granny)
My cousin Shawn
My mother Elva "Ms. Boodie Gilmore"
My wife Nina Roberts
And last and always first, GOD!

INTRODUCTION

I decided to write this autobiography a few days after my prison sentence. One morning I just woke up and could not believe all of the things that occurred in a ninety-day time frame.

I was so lost, hurt, and emotionally drained from my trial to the guilty finding, then the lies and deceit from so-called friends and family that I had to get it out. Instead of lashing out in a negative way toward COs (correctional officers) or other inmates, I wrote my thoughts and feelings down on paper.

I am one small voice for millions of women and men behind the wall who all feel or felt my pain of abandonment, confusion, hurt, loss, helplessness. We keep a smile on our face, but we cry on the inside for never wanting to seem weak or vulnerable. But we, too, are human and need someone to talk to or cry out to without being judged or looked down upon.

Every day after my sentence of eighty years, I kept a smile on my face.

I had brothers come to me—some young, some old—and tell me that I was their inspiration. Because if I could hold my head high and keep smiling with eighty years, then they could do the same with the little time they may receive. Only if they knew that all the praise they gave me actually motivated me to smile every day when I really wanted to cry.

I named this book *Buried Alive* because once you are found guilty, that is how society sees you—dead! Family, friends, associates—all tend to lose interest in you once they know you will not be home anytime soon or if ever.

This is my book, my life—unedited. So if some words are spelled incorrectly, just know that I am not illiterate. I just couldn't afford for someone to edit it, but I am sure you will understand all that I am saying and trying to achieve with this book.

This book is for the many people who want to know the truth about that day on August 30, 2019. For the people who thought they knew me or my background. For the men and women behind the prison wall who are not giving up the good fight, the fight to be free and feel alive again—not to just exist, but to live!

We refuse to be buried alive!

Davon Roberts

Some Birthday Gift

I rolled over. Hmmm, don't feel much of a difference. As I got up out of my bunk—*crack*! Yup, my damn back. I feel it now—old age.

Today is October 5, 2021, my forty-sixth year on this earth. My b-day, Boss Day, G-Day, or however you would like to call it. I just know I am another year older, and my body was reminding me of it.

Besides today being that special day that we all tend to go out of our way to celebrate each year, today was also my sentencing day.

Two counts of second-degree attempted murder…those were the charges that I was found guilty of on July 28, 2021, and now today was judgment day.

I woke up light-headed. What time is it? 4:40 a.m. Damn, I just went to sleep one hour ago—it felt longer than that. I got up to take a shower; It's the best time to do so at (MTC) Metropolitan Transition Center here in Baltimore, Maryland. The city turned this place into a pretrial facility ever since the feds came in and shut down (BCDC) Baltimore City Detention Center.

I took showers at this time of the morning because MTC has eight dorms with one hundred men per dorm, so most of the men were asleep at this time of the morning, which meant more hot water, and most of all, a sense of privacy.

After a thirty-minute shower I got dressed, brushed down my waves, and looked at myself in my makeshift mirror made out of an old plastic mirror and some tape. Hmmm…not bad-looking to be forty-six years old.

I sat on my bunk and fell into my own thoughts. Wondering what today held, how much time would the judge give me, who would come to support me—my mother, Nina, Peedy, the female who betrayed me for a so-called homeboy—so many thoughts.

About 6:00 a.m. the CO called my name over the loudspeaker in the dorm. "Davon Roberts, B23, come to the door properly dressed with your ID and mask. You have court."

I got up, dapped up a few brothers, Li'l Tado from my Hood (Cherry Hill), Chimmy from Hoffman, and a few other guys. They gave me their blessings and good lucks. Down to intake I headed.

I got to the black gate of intake. CO Smith let me in. "Good morning, Roberts," CO Smith said to me. I said good morning back to him. Smith was an old-school CO. Don't bother no one; respect him, and he will respect you. He just wanted to do his eight-hour shift and go home.

"I see you have court today, Roberts. What you got going on down there?" I told Smith that today was my sentencing day. Smith told me he wished me luck. I told him thank you, then I went to the waiting room to watch TV and wait for transportation to come and get me.

As I was watching Fox 45 News, my stomach started to bubble. Damn, I have the bubble guts. Nerves of steel just went out the window—shit just got real!

By time I came out of the bathroom, transportation was there to take me to court. The one transportation CO for Circuit Court was a guy with a gold tooth and from the Islands. Fake ass player, but cool as a fan, he said, "Hey, Rob." (Short for Roberts.) "I see you go for sentencing today. You got that crazy red hair judge who likes to give guys the max when they are found guilty."

I replied real calm like, "Yeah, I know."

My stomach really started turning. I was farting and everything. Still had my poker face on though.

The CO said, "Come on. Let me strip search you, so we can get out of here."

I hate this part of the process: strip search and that damn three-piece. If you don't know, the three-piece consisted of handcuffs, shackles, and a chain around your waist. It's hell trying to walk in this get up, and the rumor is an inmate helped invent this—wow!

My worst fear has always been being trapped in this transportation van in a fire or water in this three-piece and not able to get out. The protocol for the correctional officers is they must not let you out. Scary thought, huh?

As we rode to the courthouse, which was only five minutes from MTC, the COs put on 92Q, a local station we all love in Baltimore. I heard the music playing, but I wasn't mentally there. My thoughts were all over the place.

Once inside the bullpen of the Mitchell Court House, I was the only inmate at the time. I was pacing back and forth. I hate coming to court; nothing good ever happens. A young brother named BG came in. I was down JCI pretrial with him. He was starting his trial today. I gave him my blessings.

A few moments later, a cat out of my era named Angola came in. Real humble guy—well-respected throughout the city.

We all talked a few about law, etc. Angola and I talked about Cherry Hill and how we was at the same fish fry we had down by Harbor Hospital. I was engulfed in the conversation when the phone rang, and they called my name.

"Roberts, they're ready for you in room 203 with Judge Schiffer Chambers."

My mouth got dry. I said, "I'm ready" through dry spit. My mouth was so dry from being nervous that I drank two cartons of water and I still had cottonmouth.

I walked into the courtroom. I saw my loved ones sitting there, looking just as nervous as I was. My mother was there, Nicole, Ms. Shelia, Nina—Nina actually wore a Happy Birthday, Davon shirt for me—very nice, Jester. Toya was there, and the female that was my fiancée at the time sat next to my mother. The sight of everyone made me feel loved.

I sat next to my lawyer, Mr. Tomko. He gave me a nonchalant "good morning." I looked at the judge then over at the prosecutor. I knew this court date was serious because normally the COs remove the three-piece. They may leave the leg irons on, but the cuffs and the chain around your waist would be removed—not this morning.

The prosecutor did as he did usually—made me sound like a monster, a right out thug, then he recommended a ninety-year sentence. My lawyer, Mr. Tomko, was brief in my defense. I could tell he just wanted this to be over with. My mother got up and spoke on my behalf, Ms. Shelia (my friend Hanky's mother), then my fiancée spoke up for me.

Finally I had a chance to speak. Through tear-filled eyes, I addressed everyone from the prosecutor, my lawyer, and the victims. It was hard because my eyes were still watery from the speech my mother had given. She damn near got on her knees and begged the judge.

After all of this, the judge looked down at me with a half smirk on her face and said,

"Mr. Roberts, I'm giving you thirty years for each account of second degree attempted murder and another twenty years for use of a firearm in a crime to all run consecutive, for a total of eighty years."

I felt hot, a little light-headed. For a brief moment, I felt like Larenz Tate when he played in the movie *Dead Presidents* when the judge gave him life, and he threw the chair at the judge, but that would have been too dramatic. Plus, I still had on the three-piece, so throwing a chair was not possible.

So I just grinned, said, "Thank you, your honor," looked over at the prosecutor and said, "Good job. I look forward to seeing you on my appeal," looked at my mother, winked my eye to let her know that I am okay, walked out of there, and said to myself,

"Hell of a birthday gift."

CHAPTER 1

Cherry Hill

It Takes a Village to Raise a Child

October 5, 1975—I was born into this world to a young nineteen-year-old woman named Elva Gilmore, but better known to everyone as Ms. Boodie. My father's—better known as a sperm donor—name was John Jesse Roberts. Some called him Bo.

I was brought home from the University of Maryland Hospital, where I was born, to a place that would raise me and I would call home for the next forty-six years:

Cherry Hill.

Cherry Hill was a small urban hood located in South Baltimore. It is mostly made up of low-income housing/families. Surrounded by water and just minutes from the inner harbor, Cherry Hill was notoriously known for its violence, and rival neighborhoods never wanted to come through Cherry Hill because it was only two ways to enter—either Westport end, or Hanover Street Bridge end.

My first residence was in the 2700 block of Spelman Road. It was a two-bedroom apartment that belonged to my grandmother, Dixie Louise Brown, better known to everyone as Ms. Brown.

It was a small apartment, but it was a lot of love here. My uncle HK lived here as well. He is my mother's youngest brother. He thought he was a young Michael Jackson with his big afro, a style they wore in the '70s. My uncle would watch me from time to time, but I mostly was tucked away under my granny's fat arms—a safe haven for me, and Granny didn't play about her man, a nickname she gave me.

My mother was young and vibrant, full of life—standing six feet, slim, smooth light brown skin with a pretty smile and an open face, gold crown on her side tooth, and very loud and outspoken—everyone noticed her, even the man that raised me and I called my father, Melvin L. Bomar, better known as *Big Bomar*.

Dad, as I called him, had chased my mother since the early age of twelve, thirteen years old. I remember my mother telling me stories about how Dad used to stop, pass her paper routes, and pull her pigtails, a hairstyle she used to wear.

It got so bad that the man all the kids delivered papers for—Officer Murdock—would chase Dad away whenever he came around to taunt my mother.

In the coming years, Dad enlisted in the Army, as most young men did in those days, in hopes of coming home to a better life. Uncle Sam sold a lot of black men a false dream. While Dad had left to fight the good fight, my mother met a guy named John Roberts, better known to all as Bo.

Bo was twenty-three years old. Dude had the Billy Dee looks and hair to match. He would drive around in his fake love machine van, and he swept my mother off of her feet. The smooth voice and charm—my eighteen-year-old mother was not ready for such a guy, slick and corny all wrapped up in one.

My mother and Bo never were in an official relationship. They dated a few times, and *BOOM*, here I am. I only met Bo three, maybe four times in my entire life. Last time I'd seen him, I was about six years old, and he gave me twenty dollars for school, but that's neither here nor there.

Great thing is a few months after I was born, my father, Melvin Lee Bomar Jr., came back from the Army. When he laid eyes on my mother again, even with me in her arms, it was love at first sight all over again.

One day my mother, Dad, and my aunt Dot (that's Dad sister) were all sitting around the table, talking and laughing. Dad got up and excused himself. He told everyone that he was on his way to Dan

Brothers (a very popular shoe store at that time—still is amongst the older crowd). As Dad was about to leave, my mother said, "Take your son with you." Dad turned around, picked me up, and put me on his shoulders. I was his boy, and he carried me on his shoulders my entire life! I love you, Dad!

My mother and dad were now as one, and no man or woman could break that body of love/bond—I mean *no one*! They were young, wild, and in love. Yeah, they had up and downs just like any couple who was in a relationship, but they loved one another hard! Dad was about family, and he would always stress the importance of family. And he had no problem knocking out a cat who dared say anything crazy to his son or woman.

Growing up in the '80s, I had it all. I was the only child until my little brother, Li'l Melvin, was born in 1986. So I had every new toy out (GI Joe, Atari, Voltron, The Green Machine Big Wheel, The Animal Truck). I even had a motorcycle—you name it, I had it! All the kids would flock to my house to play with me, even if it was only for the toys.

All of my uncles were getting money (Uncle Darren, Poogy, Tony King), so they all spoiled me, especially my grandmother—her man wanted it, then her man got it.

In elementary school (#164), I dressed like a rich prince. Lambskin coat with hat to match—had it. Domino boots, leather coats, and pants—had it. Knicker Bocker shorts with the dress shoes—I rocked them, I even had the gold initials "DR" on my lens of my glasses. I had it all as a kid.

Cherry Hill was a big playground when I was coming up. Cherry Hill was split into two main sections: up the hill and down the hill, and even though there were multiple streets and individual hoods throughout down the hill and up the hill, everyone knows that the two main areas that represent it are down the hill and up the hill.

For down the hill, it was Coppin CT. And for where I am from, up the hill, it was VA, short for Veronica Avenue. I lived 937 Joplea Avenue, and the entire area was family. We was a whole village.

We had the Johson Family (Ms. Loretta, David, Dexter, Derrick, Pee-Wee, Tonya, Deek, Gleek, Craig Peety, Danielle), Ms. Julib and her family (Bruce, Monica, Lee-Lee, Mhuggy, Webb, Calvin), the Powell Family (Peebies, Roxanne, Roshell, Mann), the Shaws (Woody, Keith, Bird, Troy), the Gasque (Poochie, Mike-Mike, Ms. Climatine, Tim), the Frasier (Pam, her sister Darlene, their kids Monique, Tracy, Niecey, Dontae), Mr. Dennis and his sons (Manny, Tanky, Wealse), Mr. Timmy's kids (Lil Timmy and Dawn), Ms. Missy's kids (Malik and Khalila), Funk, T.T., Rubin, Rudy, Turk, Nell, Boo-Boo, Babygirl, Peedy, Funny, Fonzo, Anthony and Kahreem, Muffin, Kizzy, Tira, Girl Pee-Wee, Dirty David, Ronnie Baily, Tyrone Wilson, Ronnie and Johnny, Sem and Ms. Bernie, Green Eye Eric and sister Taresa, Tammy Craig and Elain and Michelle, Fat Bo, Black Corey, Flat head Derrick, Rusty, Nick and Gary, Boo and his sisters, Mario and Tyrone Pinkney, Davon Russell.

That's just to name a few—so many more that made up VA. We was a village, family!

The Cleas (Mr. Clea, Tyrone, Lonzo, Ray), Jop Blow, Meka, and her sister, Niecey.

Thank you all for the memories.

I say this all the time—we respected our elders back then. If Ms. Rose said turn that music down, I would say, "Yes, ma'am." We were kids just being kids, and we stood in a child's place.

We would enjoy outside. I never wanted to be inside. I went everywhere from clay mountain to red pond to snowballs at Mr. Mack's truck to watching the older cats scooter and Danny Boy get money over by Li'l Bra bus. Flip on dirty mattresses outside, hit bowlegged Rodney's pigeon coup. Changing my clothes three time a day because I wanted to be like Black Corey; he thought he was Big Daddy Kane.

I learned so much from people up in VA. We had gangsters (John White, Joe Edison). We had Robin Hood (Fat Bo). I was a kid, a Sponge. My childhood friend gave me my first nickname. Okay, let me clear this up—my friend Rubin (RIP Ruben) gave me the name crazy Davon. Here's how it happened.

I was the only child, so my mother used to call me in the house before it got dark. "Davon." "Davon!" "Davon, get in this house." I would never go in because I wanted to stay out and play. My friends had older brothers, so their mother allowed them to stay out later—only two, maybe three hours longer, but when you're young, you don't want to miss nothing.

So I would never go in when my mother would call me, but once my friends went in the house for the night, now I was left outside and afraid of the butt whipping that I knew I would get, so I would run away for days—bad idea. Back in the '80s child abuse was at an all-time high and DSS (Department of Social Service) investigated everything, so DSS figured I was running from something at home—wrong.

So they sent me to thirty-day inpatient centers like Walter P. Carter, etc. That's when crazy Davon was given to me, a name I lived up to in my entire youth and young adult life—crazy Davon (=) equals…*stupidity*!

Chapter 2

Granny

Life Will Never Be the Same

It was 1989, and I was in this group home in Durham, Connecticut. It was called Lake Grove at Durham. I had been in this placement for well over a year now. DSS (Department of Social Service) had sent me here by convincing my mother that it would be good for me. Plus, they felt as though I wouldn't run away from here due to the distance. They figured that would discourage me—wrong!

When I first arrived at Lake Grove, it was around April 1988. I was twelve years old. I got there around 7:00–8:00 p.m., and the kids were having their evening recreation that consisted of snacks and music. When I entered the room with the staff named Jane, all eyes turned toward me. I hated that type of attention (new kid on the block).

I was nervous as hell, but very confident. Why wouldn't I be? I had on my favorite black and burgundy velour sweat suit, a pair of white Lottos (tennis shoes), and my fake gold rope chain with the big BMW medallion with the clear nail polish on it (to stop the fake gold from fading off). On top of that I was from Baltimore. Enough said—I felt fly!

The first person to approach me was a girl name Chasity Veasle—short hair, pigeon-toed with big pretty brown eyes, and she was from Baltimore as well. We talked for a few minutes back and forth with questions for one another until her boyfriend—some white kid named Paul—put an end to all conversation. I think she likes me.

Lake Grove was made up of several cottages. I was in a co-ed one with a locked door called Lexington. A few cottages had unlocked doors. Some was all boys and all girls. The kids here were from states close by. There was kids from New York, New Jersey, a few of us from Baltimore, but the majority of the kids was Connecticut. (Danbury, Bridgeport, Hartford, etc.).

The most popular girl in my cottage was Jennifer Carney. She was fifteen years old, a white girl with dirty blond hair. She was cool as a fan. She adopted me as her little brother—even hooked me up with her younger sister who was my age. Had a picture of her and all; I was balling.

I hooked up with a kid named Sean Gamboa-Vesquz. I guess he was Hispanic (going off of his name), but he looked like a white boy with curly hair. Try to picture the actor Mark Walhborn with curly hair—yeah, he looks like him.

He was fifteen years old as well, and we hung out everywhere together. He thought he was a ladies' man. I guess now looking back on it, he did have a few of the girls there. I had a few myself—not tooting my own horn of anything. Outside of finger popping a girl, I never had sex, but Sean helped change that.

One day we all decided we was fed up with the staff at Lake Grove, and we ran away (my specialty). It was five of us (Sean, three girls: Conswela, Mary, Stacy, and myself). We all broke out with no real plan. We just ran like hell. We ended up in a dark cornfield about two hours later. We sat around bored, hungry, and scared.

Sean, being the oldest out all of us, took the so-called leader position. We talked, laughed, and fake planned. Then the conversation came up—sex! Sean asked who was a virgin? Stacy, a thirteen-year-old girl, said she was. Everyone else said they had sex before. Even I said I did, but you know I was lying like hell.

So Sean pulls me to the side and says, "Look, it's two of us and three of them." He wanted Conswela. She was fourteen years old and from Baltimore. All that was left was Mary and Stacy. Mary was a fat girl from New York, cute and nice, but Stacy was my crush. She was an Italian girl with short hair, braces on her teeth, and a mean suntan. Yeah, I'll take her.

We were all in this cornfield. Sean and Conswela were going at it like jackrabbits. I'm scared to death with all that noise Conswela was making—what the hell? But after a few minutes had passed, it was Stacy's and my turn (Little ding-a-ling, don't fail me now!).

Stacy pulled her pants down. I got dizzy. Everyone was looking, waiting—my turn. Pants came down, and I was ready. I climbed on top of her and went to insert myself into her. "Ouch! You in the wrong hole!" I was confused—how many holes was down there? But all I could say was "I know. I just wanted to make sure you was ready."

She grabbed me and inserted me into her. I heard her ouches and moans, but I was in heaven. I was moving like never before—straight jackrabbit…then *boom*, that feeling. It didn't feel the same when I done it to myself. I heard birds. I had sex with Stacy three times that night, chasing that same feeling, my new drug. A few months shy of turning thirteen years old, and I was now king.

We got caught by the police one day later, but when I got back to Lake Grove, I was not little Davon anymore. I had a serious appetite and I ran through that compound like wildfire.

A year had passed. It was 1989. I was a teenager. I had met a lot of friends—some moved back home, or to other group homes. I really never thought about when would I leave. I was thirteen years old and enjoying this change. I guess I was growing into my own.

One day one of the staff called me into the office. They was being extra nice to me. I liked this treatment; what's going on? Jane looked down at me. I liked Jane Kaplan. She used to bring her black Labrador dog named Barney with her to work every day.

Jane pulled me to her and said, "Your grandmother passed away."

I felt an anger like I never felt before. How could she do this to me? Granny told me to be good, so I could come home with her, and I had kept my end of the deal. I was being good, but she didn't keep her end of the deal.

I lost my best friend, my granny—the one who would protect me, hug me, tell me I was smart and handsome. She left me. I felt abandoned, lost… I was in shock, mad at the world. From this day on, *no one* would be able to tell me anything—I don't want to hear it.

The staff at Lake Grove put me on a plane back to Baltimore to attend my grandmother's funeral. I was supposed to return three days later. I walked in March funeral home on Wabash Avenue over West Baltimore to see my grandmother. Upon seeing her in that casket, I cried on the inside for her, but around all these strangers which was her sisters and family from North Carolina where she was born and raised, I would not cry openly around them.

I had no answers, I never felt this way before—so much anger! The day before I was to return to Connecticut to Lake Grove, I told my mother I would be right back. I never did return to Lake Grove. I had that chip on my shoulder. My heart was cold now…

Life was never the same.

CHAPTER 3

Love of My Life

Love Is Patient, Love Is Kind

It was very hard on me, dealing with the loss of my grandmother as well of the up and downs of being a teen. By 1990 I had been expelled from several schools in Baltimore City (Southern High, Francis M. Wood). The next stop would have been Harbor City, but my aunt had a better plan for me.

My aunt Delores Jones, better known to everyone as Dee Dee, was a few years older than my mother. She had no kids of her own, but always called me her son (I did look just like her). My aunt had married a guy named Bey Brother—hell of an uncle to me, good man.

The both worked for NASA out in Beltsville, Maryland, but they lived in Baltimore County, Woodlawn. Now Woodlawn, Maryland, was a great county in the '90s. Schools were top-notch. Woodlawn was a middle-class county for working families, mostly black families.

My aunt suggested that my mother allow me to come live with her and my uncle for the summer in hopes of me meeting new kids, so I would know people when I started school at Woodlawn High that September. Sounded like a plan to me. I was cool with it.

I arrived out Woodlawn, June of 1990. It was different, the people were nice, it was quiet at night, and very clean. I had so much fun. I bumped into an old Cherry Hill friend on the basketball court one day. His name was Jamaine, but we all called him Poppy Eye Jamaine because he had big eyes. He lived in Town & Country Apartments with his mother, but we always would see one another at the basketball court at Woodmore Middle School. Jamaine introduced me to a lot of people out there—especially the females.

Security Mall was one of my favorite hangout spots while I lived in Woodlawn. One day me and my friend Tuson (he was from Appleton & Mosher St.) was at Security Mall just hanging out. This girl with long hair past her shoulders (all real too), red bone, slim— her name was Antonette, and she was from Randallstown (an area ten minutes up the street from Woodlawn).

Antonette was cool, nice girl, but it was the girl who was with her, the one sitting on the bench all alone away from us all—very, very shy! I asked Antonette, "Who is that girl?"

Antonette said, "Oh, her. That's Deidre."

Deidre Moss was her name, five feet, four inches tall, light brown skin, big full lips, smart, way before her time. Deidre was two years younger than me. I fell in love. Deidre and I would talk on the phone for hours—me mostly talking, and her laughing and listening. We had become best friends.

Deidre was younger than me, but I learned so much from her. Her morals and principles were intact for real. We grew together over the years. We officially became a couple in October 1990, and I changed her last name ten years later on October 2000 to Deidre Roberts!

By then Deidre had graduated from Bowie State University, and we had moved in Woodridge Apts. which is out in Randallstown, Maryland. We was twenty-three and twenty-five years old. We were young and thought we were grown, but we were still kids in all reality.

I will admit it now, I was not ready to be a husband, I was in love with Deidre and I wanted to be with her forever but I did not understand what being a husband meant. To be honest, I got worse.

I'd been taking Deidre thru hell for years—major cheating! I mean since we was in our teens. She was so patient with me. She just wanted me to change. She used to tell me that my loyalty was more to Cherry Hill and those streets, and I would always deny it, but looking back on it, she was right.

I hurt Deidre. It was nights I would wake up, and she would be sitting up in the bed looking at me, and I would say, "What's wrong with you?" Sounding all stupid, and she would say, "Did you sleep with that girl in the apartment next door?"

Me sounding stupid again. "No!" But wondering to myself, *how did she know that?*

I learned a lot about women from Deidre—things a lot of us men don't know or care to ask women about.

From small things like a woman's time of that month—overnight pads with the wings because her cycle is heavy to not sitting completely in the tube because can get yeast infections to something major as not feeling like a complete woman because you think you can't have kids.

See, I thought it was Deidre being dramatic on her Mary J. Blidge stuff. But for years she was trying to get pregnant and couldn't. Her friends had married and became pregnant, but not her. We went to fertility clinics, put pillows under her butt after sex, so nothing would spill out. We both even took vitamins—counted ovulation times each month, and still nothing for years.

This played on her mental, and since I already had a son, she blamed herself—depression mode. I wasn't any help either because even though I had never been caught cheating, my actions was showing otherwise—coming in late nights, hiding my cell phone—all the telltale signs of a cheater!

With all that Deidre was going through mentally, she still was so patient, humble, kind, and loving toward me. She asked me one day, "If you love me so much, why do you hurt me the way you do?"

I looked at her all stupid again and I honestly had no answer. I had never been caught cheating and I swore I was a good husband, so what is she talking about? Only a real man would understand her question—I didn't understand it until years later.

This woman had been through the ringer and back with me. From leaving high school at seventeen years old just to catch several buses and subways to come all the way to MCI-J in Jessup for night visits, and she was only seventeen years old. We would beg the CO to let her in because a person had to be eighteen years old to visit an inmate, and she would come that long way not even knowing if that CO would let her in, so from Randallstown to Jessup she would come.

Deidre had done so many prison bids with me from Hickey School to Boys Village to MCTC, EHU, RCI, MCI-J, BCCC, MTC, BPRU, popular Hill Pre-Release to BrockBridge. She is loyal—a real woman—and I realize age does not make a woman or man.

We eventually had a son, Davon Roberts Jr. born on September 11, 2005. I nicknamed him Man-man because my grandmother used to call me man. Deidre went into full Mommy/wife mode. She felt complete now, but I still was silly. Loyalty was more to Cherry Hill and the streets, even still cheating. I got locked up in 2006 for something I didn't even do.

My codefendant Asim Benns AKA Sim and I got locked up for attempted murder because some guy from Cherry Hill mentioned our name because he got locked up for drugs and wanted a way out. So lie on me and Sim is what he did. That's why they call him Sucker Type.

Thank God that the person that was shot knew me and Sim and told those people the truth: that we was not the ones who shot him. The case was thrown out, and we was set free, except Sim had a probation violation, so they sent him to BPRU (Balto Pre-Release Unit).

While I was over BCDC (Balto., City Detention Center), a house that Deidre and I applied for came through. It was for first-time home buyers. The program was the Nieahmyah program. The home could not be over $190,000. We found a nice two-bedroom, one and a half bathroom, one-car garage and basement. It sat on one anchor of land. When I left out of BCDC in May 2007 and got in the car with Deidre and our son (who was going on two years old), Deidre turned to me and said, "Let's go, Davon. I don't want you dead in these streets. Don't ever look back." I said, "Okay, bae," and up 83 North we headed!

Love is patient.

CHAPTER 4

New Beginnings

York, Pennsylvania. You Look for Trouble You'll Find It

May 2007, York, Pennsylvania, Springettsbury Township. My ex-wife Deidre found us a nice home outside of York City, we were in York County off of Market Street right around the corner from the York Gallery, down the street from the Walmart and a nightclub called Fat Daddy's.

When I first arrived at home it felt so good. I was used to the county atmosphere because we had lived in Ellicott City, Maryland, and other counties, but York County was different.

We sat on our deck that first night of me being home. Our son, Man-Man, was upstairs asleep. We talked about life, the opportunities York, Pennsylvania, offered, and us starting over as a family—the talk felt so good along with the quietness of that night. I felt everything that Deidre and I talked about.

First things first, I needed a job. Before I got locked up in 2006, I was doing my thing in Brooklyn, Maryland, but since being over that jail for those eight months, a lot had changed.

My gold 2005 Chevy Impala had been repo-ed, funds had dried up a lot, a few good men had hit me off with some money when I got out (Fleet, Peedy, Lano), and I appreciated that, but by time I brought some new clothes and some food for the house, I was broke again.

I searched high and low for a job. I shared cars with Deidre; I would drop her off at work, then our son at nanny daycare, and off

I went, job hunting like a good old husband, frustrated as hell. In the process of job hunting, I started learning all about Pennsylvania (Harrisburg, York, Lancaster, Steelton, Red Loin, etc.). If it was located near York, Pennsylvania, I was there, but I also was meeting people as well—not always a good thing.

First things first, I needed my own car because sharing this car with my wife was putting me on a tight schedule. I would only be out for a few hours then I would have to be back to pick Deidre and Man-Man up—not cool. I go down to Market Street one day to this used car dealership—some crappy dealer too, but he had a car that I've always loved. I'd seen nothing else on his lot but this one car.

It was an all-black with burgundy leather 1998 Chevy Caprice. I loved this car. I felt free again; no more sharing cars, no more having to rush back home. The body was in good shape, so was the inside. I don't remember how many miles was on the dash, but it was not that high. But lo and behold, the engine was not up to my pushing it as hard as I was used to pushing vehicles, but it was cool.

Off I went, up and down 83, from Harrisburg to Baltimore I ran day and night. I was back to my old ways, hustling, late nights, and yup, you guessed it…cheating! These cities were not ready for me. I moved fast but friendly. I had something that Harrisburg, Lancaster, and York loved—that Dog Food!

Dog Food is street name for a drug: heroin. I am from Baltimore where we specialize in heroin, and we have plenty of it! But in Harrisburg, Lancaster, and York, Pennsylvania, they was stingy with it. Our heroin users would have killed someone in Pennsylvania for the small quantities they sold in Harrisburg, Lancaster, and York, Pennsylvania. It was ridiculous, but me seeing this, I saw an opportunity.

I decided to hit them with our triple O gel caps which would go for ten dollars down in Baltimore, but easily twenty-five dollars in Pennsylvania. I even went 50/50 (except for shorts) with the person I had selling for me. They lost their mind; no one went 50/50 anymore, except for me. In all reality, my heroin was actually being sold for free for me—one hundred percent profit. We all was good.

No one knew my name except for my ex-wife, and she did not know none of my associates. Everyone in Pennsylvania called me B-more, short for Baltimore.

I met some real men in Harrisburg, Lancaster, and especially York, Pennsylvania. I met a lot of women; they loved the accent. They would all ask me to say "Two." LOL, yeah, okay.

I met this one female from Harrisburg. We meshed very well—a little too well. She wasn't even from Harrisburg, but she was a sexy young gangster. A few months running things was cool, except at home. I was not a good husband. Deidre's attempt to better me for our family had failed. I wanted my cake and ate it too. I loved my wife and children, but I loved the streets as well.

One day a Spanish guy called me to Harrisburg to pick up some money he owed me and to get some more of that Dog Food. Me and a cat I messed with who was from North Philly (6th and Diamond) respectfully, whose name was Shizz (My man one hundred grand).

So Shizz and I got to Harrisburg. We met the Spanish guy. He gave me the money. We made small talk. He got his Dog Food.

As Shizz and I headed back to our destination, a white van pulled up beside us. This was a scene out of a movie. The officer leans out of the side of the van with guns drawn. The guy who was digging in the trash—who we thought was homeless—*boom*, was a cop. We was on the ground before we knew what hit us. Yeah, the Spanish guy set us up.

We were on our way to DCP (Dauphin County Prison) which was in Harrisburg, Pennsylvania. After a few days in, a detective came to visit me. "Mr. Roberts, we was wondering when we would find out who you were."

"Huh?" I said. My face came up in a bank robbery from a few months prior.

Remember that gangster female I had met in Harrisburg? Well, she got caught for a bank robbery, but they wanted to know who was the driver. She said, "B-More." At the time, I had never been locked up in Pennsylvania before, so there was no mug shot to show her.

Now that I was locked up for the drug charge, they had a mug shot. "Sir, I have no idea what you are talking about. I hack people around every day for money. I don't know nothing about a bank robbery."

The detective smiled at me and said, "Yeah, okay."

I ran back to call my wife Deidre. She was crying! "Bae, what is wrong?" I asked her.

"Davon, all these detectives ran up in this house looking for stuff. They took the computers. They talking about you robbed a bank. I thought you told me you got locked up for drugs!"

Me with the stupid answer again. "They talking about something old, bae."

Two weeks later, they called me up for legal mail. They were divorce papers. They was filed on February 14, 2008, yup, on Valentine's Day! I messed up this time. I learned you can take a person out of their town, city, hood, or state, but if they change their way of thinking, they will be good. But if they don't change their way of thinking, they will get the same results—trouble!

If you look for trouble, you will find it!

CHAPTER 5

2017: I'm Back

Blonde Bombshell

March 2017, I'm back. I'm free. After just doing nine and a half years in prison, I was finally free—well, not totally free yet. I was in a halfway house in Wernerville, Pennsylvania. Wernerville was a town that sat outside of Reading, Pennsylvania.

I had to do nineteen days in this halfway house before they felt as though I was fully ready to enter back into society. I had lost a lot since 2008. Of course, I lost my marriage, and even though Deidre and I were divorced for those nine and a half years, she still brought my son to see me on visits—faithfully!

I had lost nine and a half years of time—nine and a half years of my life that I could not regain back. Nine and a half years out of both of my sons' lives—so much had changed.

While incarcerated, I had met my brother from another mother, Darrlyn Stanton AKA Dizzy. He was from Baltimore, but had made Philly his home. Most of his family was located in Philly and Norristown, Pennsylvania. We immediately clicked and hit it off when he got to the prison that I was located in.

We worked out together, ate, laughed, planned, and built with one another daily. If I didn't know any better, I would have thought we had the same fathers. We was so much alike.

Dizzy was due to be released a few months before I was. We went extra hard in that weight pit. I was six feet, three inches tall, 250 pounds. Nice! One day, Dizzy was on the phone, and I asked who he was talking to. He said his sister, Pumpkin. Just being polite I said, "Tell her that I said hello,"

I had remembered her from his family pictures that he had showed me. He told me to tell her myself.

So I got on the phone and said, "Hello, Ms. Pumpkin."

She said, "Who is this?"

I said, "Davon."

She said, "Oh. Hello!"

Every time I would see Dizzy on the phone with her, I would jump on just to say hi until one day she stopped me and said, "Davon, how old are you?"

I said, "Forty-one years old."

She said, "Well, you are older than me. Why do you keep calling me miss?"

I said, "Just being polite." She smiled (I could tell through the phone).

Another week or so passed. She stopped me on the phone. "Are you single, Davon?"

"Yes, I am. Are you?" I asked.

"Yes," she responded, then she said, "By the way, my name is Nicole."

From that moment, we was on the phone daily—several times a day.

Nicole Jones-Randall was her name. 5'9 tall, every bit of 220 pounds. All hips and thighs, light brown skin, cute smile with the gold tooth on her front, and big pretty eyes. Yeah, I was open. She asked me what were my plans when I got released in a few weeks. I told her I had to do ninety days in the halfway house, but I may stay longer to save money and get me a place somewhere in Reading, Pennsylvania. She never mentioned it again. No questions or anything about my release. I would learn later on her mind was made up already; I just didn't know it.

My man Dizzy had left a few weeks before me. He was in the halfway house in Philly. Stunning with the ladies, sending me pics, we talking on the three-way. I missed my bro, but I was happy he was free—three and a half weeks to go for me.

I got my release clothes sent in an all-black sweatsuit and a pair all-white Nike Airs (three quarter with the strap). My childhood friend, Malik, AKA DJ Mello sent me my clothes. He made sure I was good. Malik is family for real.

We would be called to the property room a week before our release to try on our release clothes, so just in case we can't fit them, our family has enough time to send us in more that will fit. My stuff fit perfectly. I went back to my housing unit, pumped up. It felt good to put on some real clothes after nine and a half years. I was ten days from my release.

I jumped on the phone to call my new crush, Nicole. She had just gotten off of work. I told her I had tried my release clothes on and I felt good. She said, "That's nice."

Then she asked me to get a pen and to write down this number. I wrote down the number as she said it, a little confused. I asked, "What is this number for?"

She said, "It's your conformation number for your bus ticket I brought for you. I want you to come to Baltimore first, then we will get you to the halfway house." As long as you were in the halfway house before midnight, you was good. I was speechless. All I could say was thank you!

The day had finally come. After nine and a half years, I was on my way back to Baltimore. I was excited, overwhelmed. It felt as though everything was in slow motion. The bus was moving so damn slow. I was on my way down 95 south toward Baltimore. The new bus station on Russell Street was not there in 2008 when I left; it was located next to the new Horse Shoe Casino. So much had changed in nine and a half years—time waits for no one.

On the bus ride, a young lady sat next to me. We had small talk for the two-hour ride. She said, "I can tell you are just coming home. You have that prison glow. Plus, you're looking at stuff like it's all new to you." She was right; I was shining, and things did look different. Even her cell phone was difficult to operate. Of course, she wanted to help me call whoever I needed to call—LOL.

The bus came off of the highway. My stomach started turning soon as I seen Cherry Hill—I was home! I stood up to exit the bus with my one little plastic bag that had nothing but a few pictures and release papers in it. The young lady that sat next to me on the ride down gave me a hug and a kiss on the cheek told me to call her and to be safe. I was surprised as hell by her gesture, but it was nice. I never called nor seen her again.

I stepped off of the bus and seen something that brought tears to my eyes instantly. It was my mother and Dad! We hugged for hours—okay, it was only for a few minutes, but it felt like hours. I'm a mommy's boy and daddy's baby. We took pics, and my mother was ready to go. I said, "Hold on, Ma. Someone is on the way that I want for you to meet." My mother had heard about Nicole, but never met her—neither had I, outside of pictures.

I had used my father's phone to call Nicole. She answered on the first ring. First thing she said was, "I'm pulling up right now—where are you?"

Soon as I looked up, I seen the day time running lights of an all-black Lexus LS 460 pulling up beside me. We locked eyes and stared at each other through the closed window until I broke the silence and said, "Get out and give me a hug." She smiled.

She got out of the car. She had on an all-black bodysuit with a black leather jacket, these black shoes, gold bracelets, necklace, rings, and those big pretty eyes hid underneath the bangs of her wrap hairdo. The color of her hair was platinum blonde. She looked like she belonged in the LL Cool J video, "Around The Way Girl." Nicole was amazing.

We kissed, hugged, and kissed again. We both briefly forgot about my mother and Dad being there. I looked up. "Oh, Ma, this is Nicole."

Summer of 2017, Nicole and I was connected like twins. She would drive from Baltimore to Wernerville, Pennsylvania every weekend. I would get twelve and twenty-four-hour passes on the weekend, but it had to be in Pennsylvania—at least, it was supposed to be.

In May of 2017, I brought a Ford Edge Crossover, a midsize SUV. I got it from Drive Time. It was on now—my weekend passes was now in Baltimore. In June, I was released from the halfway house. Nicole and I decided I would come live with her over at East Baltimore.

Nicole had three sons (Tavon, Jamal, and Ty). Her sons were very overprotective about their mother—as they should be. I was the only man in that household since the passing of their father, so they were not feeling me. A lot of face fighting, but over time we was one big family. We was good; plus, once they seen how happy their mother was, I was now on the cool list.

One thing I can say about Nicole and my relationship—we were real friends. Even to this day we are friends. We both worked long hours. I was more of a homebody; Nicole loved to go out.

So we made it our business to have our outing every weekend. It didn't matter how much money we had in our pocket, or where we would go. We was happy—just the two of us. We would put our music on the radio and hit the highway. Of course, I was the driver. Some days we would be in Baltimore, other days we would end up in Philly or Norristown. Some days we would just chill and eat crabs—Nicole's favorite.

We was like this for a couple of years. I had moved out because I wanted a change. A lot was going on over East. We had our brief disagreement. Nothing major—we just started having different ideas of what we wanted out of life. We never grew apart; we just grew in different directions.

We grew a lot, learned a lot from one another—we are solid! I can honestly call on her as a friend, and she will show her loyalty as a friend. No, I didn't get a wife in Nicole, but I got a lifelong friend…

My blonde bombshell.

CHAPTER 6

On My Own

Loyalty Over Love

Well, here I was in 2018, doing okay, considering I only been home for a little over a year now. I was nowhere near my goals that I had set for myself a year ago while I was still incarcerated at the halfway house, but I was very proud of myself because I had given myself a real chance: no selling drugs, etc. Just working long hard hours, as a man should do.

I was driving a flatbed truck for a company in Jessup, Maryland. I would deliver slabs of marble and concrete. I loved my job. I was no longer living with Nicole which was a nightmare in the beginning because I could not find a place to live.

No, it's not because no one wanted me. I could have lived with friends or family if I needed or wanted to, but I wanted my own. Since I was young, I lived with someone" Deidre and I when I was married, then I came home in 2017 to live with Nicole. I wanted my own space, I wanted to pick out my own household goods, my touch. Call me selfish—oh well.

But it wasn't easy as I thought it would be. I had a full-time job and I had been there for almost a year. I had got my credit up to 590. Not good, but considering it was 440 when I first came home, it was on the rise—so what was the problem?

My background. Every apartment complex I applied for, they denied me due to my drug conviction, which I was still on parole for. This situation alone could be discouraging to many men and women who have served their prison time, or so-called paid their dues to society, then come home. Work hard to change and be productive, only to still be judged for their past…to the point that we couldn't even get a one-bedroom apartment.

Without support from family or friends, some would lose hope and return to that dark place of feeling helpless—which in turn can possibly have that person run to drugs, alcohol, or crime or whatever their vice may be when they become depressed or feeling alone and lost.

So here I was working fifty plus hours a week, saving my money, and trying to reestablish myself as a man instead of laying up on a woman—something my mother taught me to never do! But I couldn't even get me a one-bedroom apartment, and I refused to rent a room and share a bathroom with other roommates/house mates.

Just as I was about to give up, God sent me an angel. Her name is Nina; we had been family since we were young, but we lost contact with one another in 2006. I had moved to York, Pennsylvania, with my ex-wife, Deidre, then I was incarcerated for nine and a half years. So when I received a message from Nina in late 2017 via Facebook, I was surprised and happy to reconnect with my family.

I was talking to Nina about my current situation, and lo and behold, she had a friend who was looking to rent out their town home: a two-bedroom, one and a half bathroom, split level town-house—thank you, God!

At $1400 a month rent, I felt so good about this. If it wasn't for the help of Nina and her friend overlooking my past and only focusing on my work history, I would have been living with someone—no sense of independence whatsoever.

Over the next year or so, Nina and I had a chance to catch up with one another. I told her about my past's up and downs. She told me about her kids and why she moved back to Columbia, Maryland, from South Carolina. It was like old times; it was nice.

Things started looking up for me. I finally felt as though I was moving in the right direction. I got a new job in Jessup, Maryland, two new cars, and my own place. Of course, I met a few new female friends—I still kept in touch with Nicole as well, even though we saw each other less often no. We still found time to laugh with one another from time to time.

To be honest, this time alone did feel good. To finally be able to come home from work and chill with Mary Jane and a movie—no pressure or worries. I did not miss drama, but I missed *love*! I may sound soft, or on some Carl Thomas emotional stuff, but us—meaning us men—we are human, and even though we have that I-don't-care attitude, we love to love and be loved as well in return.

Even though I was proud to have my own and felt a great sense of accomplishment, I had many lonely nights. I may have had a warm body next to me, but I was still lonely. I substituted sex for love, company for the night for real companionship. I never felt this before. Damn, this was more than a phase…it was a yearning.

C HAPTER 7

New Love

One More Go Around—I Feel Alive Again

It was June 2019; hot as hell outside. I just got off of working at the job I once liked, but grew to dislike. They was playing games with that money. They promised me a raise with certain incentives as long as I worked hard, kept my truck out of accidents, no calling out, etc.

I kept my end of the deal up. Now it was excuses with them… wow! I got off of work mad on a mission to find me another job, stuck in my thoughts as I drove down Route 1 (Washington Blvd.) from Jessup, Maryland, toward Balto City. I needed to get home to Mary Jane, but first I have to stop at 7-Eleven in Pigtown off of MLK and Washington Blvd. to get some Dutches and some snacks for those cravings. because Mary Jane knows how to put it on me. Y'all know I ain't lying, have you eating the entire house. LOL.

I was in the line at 7-Eleven waiting for the cashier to ring me up when she walked in. She was 5'5–5'6, dark brown skin, average build. She wore a dark reddish natural hair style. Nice-looking woman, but her eyes were amazing. She looked right through my soul and me as well as if I wasn't there. LOL, I wanted to meet her though. I had to.

I now get the corny line of the year award for what I said to her once she came outside. "Where your husband at?" That was all I could think of at the time.

Her response was "I don't have one of those."

"Yes, you do now," I said boldly. I got a smile from her, gave her my cell number, and I went on home to take a shower, holler at Mary Jane, and go to sleep. I was tired from work today, and these steel toe boots had my feet hurting. I have no corns or anything, but my feet still was hurting.

I drove home. By the time I got home and through the door, a text came in. I got out of my car and went in the house, took them damn boots off, and started to roll Mary up before I got in the shower. Damn, I almost forgot—let me see who texted me. I looked at my phone. The text said, "Hey this is my # I just met you at 7-11." I smiled.

I asked her if I could call her because I'm not a big texter. She said yes and we talked. One conversation led to another one. Somehow she talked me into coming back out, and we ended up on top of Federal Hill, down by the Baltimore Inner Harbor with a bottle of wine and a lot of conversation—feet still hurting and all. Damn, I like her, stuck!

She worked late nights from 7:00 p.m. to 7:30 a.m. At the time I was still working with the company that I was unhappy with. That would change in a few weeks. Until then I would go in at 2:00 a.m., do my long-distance runs, and be back home around 2:00 p.m. hoping to reach home before she went to work at 7:00 p.m.

Days went to weeks to early morning dates: 7:30 a.m. to 8:00 a.m. breakfasts at Cracker Barrel or down on Charles St. at the Sushi Bar. We felt that spot because we would go upstairs to eat alone from everyone else—just us and good conversation.

I loved our conversations. She challenged my mind, had a lot of great ideas, and most of all, she was very outspoken, very ambitious. We had one heart-to-heart conversation that hit home for the both of us. We both was in group homes as kids, so we both could relate to the loneliness as youth. She was three years older than me, but very young at heart, good-natured.

I mentioned going back to school, and she pushed me to go. She even went to the college with me when I went to register for class, very supportive.

Our very first major event or holiday for us as a couple was her birthday. I had to do something nice for my bae. It was July 2019, and she was turning forty-seven years old. She was very private, so a big b-day bash was not in our future. Flowers—now I did that on regular days, but this day was special—her day.

I rolled up, excited for our day out. We made a stop over her mother's house over west Baltimore. I met her brother, a few of her cousins, gave her mother some flowers, and we was on our way. Up 95 North we went. About two hours later, we touched down in South Philly. Ocean Prime was the restaurant that I took her to.

She had never been to this restaurant before and enjoyed her b-day gift. We talked over sea bass and filet mignon (medium rare), truffle potatoes, spinach, a bottle of Dom. Yeah, I did that! I love her—stuck!

I felt good, alive again—no more games, eggs all in one basket, energy was good. We were on the same page, no secrets. Shared her on social media; a lot of people were happy for us. Shit felt good.

A few months passed by, and we had no problems. She was getting ready for a trip to Cancun with a friend for her friend's birthday. The trip was planned before we met, so I didn't go. Just told her to be careful, call me when she landed, and to have fun. I never met her friend, but it was some female she once worked with. It was supposed to just be the two of them, but all of a sudden, the friend's brother ends up there…oh, okay!

We talked on and off a few times while she was there, a few face times through Facebook, but sometimes she went missing in action. Cool, she on vacation. She mentioned that a lot of correctional officers was down there for some event they come to every year—oh, okay!

The day came for me to pick her up at BWI Airport. I was excited to see my bae. It's been four days, and she decided to stay one extra day after her friend had left, said she needed an extra day to chill—oh, okay!

I was at BWI Airport early, waiting for her. Flowers and balloons in hand, I was there to let her know that I missed her like hell! She exited the plane and went by me in a hurry. I called out. "Bae!"

She kept going. Finally, I called her name. She stopped. I was kind of shocked, but she said she was tired and didn't hear me—oh, okay! Something was different…

For a day or two, she was kind of distant—couldn't put my finger on it. Just a lot of phone conversation with the female she went to Cancun, a lot of mention of some CO (correctional officer) she sat on the plane with, and some of his troubles with the law she overheard him talking about on his phone while they was on the flight.

Come to find out they sat next to one another going there, and when she came back, she called to schedule an extra day to stay in Cancun, and she still ended up sitting next to the CO—oh, okay!

After a few days, we was back to our old ways—hanging out, eating, and watching Netflix (her favorite). One day she asked me if I wanted any more kids. I said I always wanted a daughter. She said she did as well. She had one son.

Due to her having a hysterectomy done, she could not carry a baby herself, so she asked me what did I think about having someone else carry the baby, but use her egg and use my sperm. I was pumped. "Let's do this" (a phrase she used to use).

Around this time, I posted an engagement ring on social media to ask the ladies what did they think about it? Ninety percent loved it. This was the ring that I would get—time to settle down; she is the one. I'm *in* love now! Stuck!

We was lying in bed one day, talking about all we had planned these last few months. She asked me if I still kept in contact with old girlfriends. I said, "Not really since we been in a relationship—why?" She just wanted to see how serious I was about our relationship. I rolled over on my side to face her and said, "I'm in love with you and I am very important about you, us, our relationship."

We made love—sound corny, huh? Well, as a man who was in love, sex wasn't just sex—it was love—stuck!

CHAPTER 8

The Lie Detector Test

"They say it's not what a person says in
your face, but what they do behind your
back to show their true character."

It had been a few weeks since she had come back from her trip to Cancun. We both went back to our daily lives—work, Netflix nights together, and quality time together. It felt good to finally have things going good for me.

I came in the house one day. No, we didn't live together, but I was over her house so much, it felt like I lived there. As I entered the house, I noticed she got up off of the couch to finish her phone call. I guess she had something dealing with work and needed some privacy.

She came from the kitchen once she was done on the phone. We started eating some food I had stopped and picked up for me—I loved chicken with the Singapore noodles, turned her on to them. After we ate, we sat down to watch *Judge Judy*—her favorite show; she turned me on to this show.

She was looking through her phone because the girl she went to Cancun with was sending her some pictures they had took while they was in Cancun. That's who she was on the phone with when I came in the house earlier, so she said.

A few pictures came through her phone that kind of surprised me—well, me saying surprised by them is an understatement—I was hurt, mad, disappointed, but I don't want to jump to conclusions, so let me ask her. "Bae, why are you on some of these pictures with your friend's brother?" It was a lot of excuses, then it was the blame game, then she said I was insecure, immature, etc. Damn, I just want to know why—no need to call me names or play the victim—red flag!

I won't lie; after that day, instead of me overlooking stuff and giving her the benefit of the doubt. I started asking a lot of questions. She didn't like that!

I would ask, "Hey, bae, why you got two phones? Bae, why this, why that?" The more I asked question, the more secretive she became. I did a major no-no one day. I looked through her phone. To be honest, I didn't find much. Damn, I'm a loser—not trusting your woman is a no-no, and she hasn't even done nothing. I got a lot of making up to her. She rubbed it in my face extra thick too—I deserved it!

A week or two passed by. She just came in from work and she would go right to the shower after work. I was on the couch reading when I heard a few sounds—*ping, ping, ping*—it was her message notification on her phone, but it was on her second phone—phone #2 that she claimed was her work phone. Somehow, I found myself getting the phone out of her work bag and looking through it. It was me being curious. Now I was noisy, but they say if you go looking for something, you will find it—damn.

The whole time I thought I was wrong. I had a true-blue woman, as she would tell me, when the whole time she was texting and emailing men, so-called old friends. Some texts was old before I had met her, but some texts was sent and received since we been together.

When she got out of the shower, I asked her about it. She flipped it on me. "Why you go through my phone? I just got off of work, I'm tired, I don't feel like talking about this! You are so insecure! So immature!"

I was everything under the sun, and the only explanation I got was "these are old friends. I'm not having sex with them."

"But I see them flirting with you and all you text back is 'LOL,' it seems like they don't know you're in a relationship."

No response. She just looked at me like I was wrong and kept saying, "Why you go through my phone?"

Then she went to why she don't need to cheat on me—I love you, I would never hurt you, I'm too old for games, I'm true blue, they are just friends, you need to trust me, etc. To be honest, I was confused. Maybe I was being insecure, I'm tripping, this woman loves me—maybe it was my guilt of cheating on my ex-wife in the past. I need to believe her!

Then she came out and said, "Bae, I am willing to take a lie detector test to show you I'm being real with you."

"Now, bae, you don't have to do that. I believe you." She smiled, then we made love. I won't lie, even though I tried to be a man about the things I seen in her second phone, I couldn't take the thought of seeing a man flirt with my woman, and all I could do was take her word for it. And even though I didn't say anything to her about it, she must have seen it in my attitude because she came out of the blue and said, "Why are you still tripping over that phone situation?" I tried to act as if something else was on my mind, but she had me red-handed. I couldn't hide it.

We went back and forth about our relationship, life, etc., She finally said it again. "I'll take a lie detector test to show you—I'm willing, I don't cheat, never have, never will."

I looked at her and said, "Okay, take a lie detector test because I need some peace of mind." She looked up at me, looked into my eyes as if trying to read me, and said, "Oh, okay, I will do it."

CHAPTER 9

The Storm

"They say you don't miss someone
until they are gone."

It was August 30, 2019. Today was a big day for me. Today was my mother's sixty-third birthday. On top of that, I had a new job opportunity as a driver for a big company located out in Fredrick, Maryland, and today I had to go get my start date and sign a few payers for my new job. I had planned to stop by my mother's house after I left Fredrick, Maryland, and take all of us out to dinner (my mother, father, my girlfriend, and myself) for my mother's birthday—you know, just a family outing.

I stopped over at my girlfriend's house to pick her up because she was going out to my new job with me, then we would stop in Laurel, Maryland, to the lie detector testing site. As my girlfriend and I rode out to Fredrick, Maryland, toward my new job. She turned toward me as I was driving and said, "When I pass this lie detector test, I feel as though we should end this relationship."

I said "why?"

Now looking back on it and getting to know her a lot better, she made that statement to me knowing I loved her deeply and never wanted to be without her, and that statement would discourage me from going through with the lie detector test, but I had to know the truth. So when I asked her, "Why?" she said, "If you don't trust me enough to take my word, why should we be together?"

I looked at her real fast because I was driving and said, "Why did you offer to take the lie detector test then?" She just looked away from me and stared out the window.

An hour later we was leaving Fredrick, Maryland, and headed toward Laurel, Maryland, to get this lie detector test over with. We had an appointment to be there by 2:30 p.m., and it was now 1:07 p.m. We made a few stops to get gas and use the bathroom. Besides that, the ride was total silence. Neither of us uttered a word. I was in my thoughts.

We arrived at the lie detector test site in Laurel, Maryland. We was greeted by a tall, slim blonde-haired woman, maybe mid to late thirties. She was the one who would be giving the test. She went over all the rules and regulations of the test and the process. She showed her certificates and told us her background. We read everything and signed the papers.

The test took about forty-five minutes. I had to leave the room, which left my girlfriend and the tester alone. I waited in the make-shift waiting area for about fifty minutes, then the tester and my girlfriend walked out. The tester said she would have the results by the end of the day, and she would call us, but send the actual results by email. My girlfriend and I said, "Thank you," and we walked out of the door of the testing site.

As we walk back toward my car, my girlfriend stopped outside of my car and said she wanted to take the Marc train back to Baltimore, Maryland, alone. I asked her why. She wouldn't answer me. I told her to get in the car; we drove out here together, so we was leaving together. Plus, I wouldn't leave her alone on a Marc train.

On the way home I stopped at Popeye's to get something to eat. I asked her did she want something to eat. She said no, she wasn't hungry, and to be honest, I don't know why because it was now around 4:45 p.m., and neither one of us had eaten all day, so I tried to make small talk, but it was the same as when we was on our way to Laurel, Maryland. Silence.

We finally arrived at her house. She said she was going upstairs to her bedroom to take a nap. She was tired. I said okay and sat down on the couch to eat the chicken strips and red beans and rice I got from Popeye's.

I sat on the couch, ate my food, and played with the TV, looking for something to watch. My phone rang and I could see by the caller ID that it was the lady's number from Laurel, Maryland, who gave us the lie detector test. I answered and started to walk up the stairs to my girlfriend's room to let her know that the lady was on the phone.

She was awake, lying on the bed. I put the phone on speaker, so we both could hear the results. There were three questions that was asked on the lie detector test.

1. Did she have any type of sexual activity with any other man since being in a relationship with Davon?
2. Do she talk to exes in hopes of having sex with?
3. Do she meet and have sex with men?

The tester read the results over the phone. "There was deception on the questions, with the highest score possible." My girlfriend started yelling at the lady on the phone, calling her a liar, and saying she was going to sue her. I felt numb, confused, hurt, angry, betrayed, lost, sad. Tears rolled down my eyes. I walked downstairs, sat on the couch in a daze—my heart was broken.

My girlfriend walked down the steps and was still yelling at the lady on the phone. I was mentally in space, so I don't remember exactly what she was saying to the lady on the phone.

She hung the phone up with the lady, and I looked at her and asked her, "Why?" We fussed back and forth for damn near an hour. She denied everything, told me the test was wrong. I wanted to leave, I was done, hurt, I wanted a blunt—my head was all over the place. I told my girlfriend that I was leaving.

She grabbed me and said "No!" because she thought I wouldn't come back, so she said she was leaving, I told her "No!" that I would come back too. There was no need for her to leave. I really was going to come back. I honestly just wanted a blunt to get my head right. If you don't smoke marijuana, you can't and won't understand the comfort it brings a person when you are stressed—I guess the same way a cigarette does for a person who smokes them. I loved my Mary Jane.

So as my girlfriend attempted to leave the house to avoid me from going out, some lady with a Pit bull dog stopped in front of the door and shouted something to me. I couldn't hear her clearly because the storm door was closed. Besides, my girlfriend and I both was crying and talking to one another in the door way.

When I opened up the front door to see what the lady with the Pit bull was saying. She started yelling for me to let my girlfriend out the door if she wanted to come out! "Huh?" I looked at this lady and said, "Mind your damn business. You don't even know what is going on—dumbass!"

Just as I said that I grabbed my girlfriend and told her, "Let's go—you can go with me." I tried to grab her by her shoulder, but I grabbed her hair. She had long plats that went down her back, so I got a hold of her hair as well of her shoulder, plus I was watching the lady and her Pit bull. As my girlfriend and I was walking toward my car to leave, the lady with the Pit bull yell out to me, "Let her go now!"

I said "Fuck you! Mind your fucking business and take that mutt home."

As I opened the passenger door, so my girlfriend could get in the car, the lady with the Pit bull was running toward me with her dog.

All I could say was, "Get that dog away from me!"

The lady said, "What you say about my dog?" My girlfriend jumped out the car toward me and the lady. The dog was barking, the lady was yelling. I had a gun in my pocket that I kept on me at all times due to the violence on the street which I kept in my car in a red lunch box. I was putting it in the trunk of my car because I was about to smoke a blunt, and I didn't want the gun in my front of the car.

As I was in my trunk and the lady was running toward me, my girlfriend seen the gun that I was taking from my pocket to put in the trunk. She grabbed my hand and the gun, and it went off. All so fast, in seconds the woman I love was shot. Everything moved in slow motion—I looked around. No one was here with me; I was scared alone. I panicked, got in my car, and drove off.

I was all over the place that night, no sleep, tossing and turning—blunt after blunt. Was she okay? I called the hospital. They confirmed she was in that hospital, but I needed a secret code from the family to talk to her. I was lost, alone, scared. For days, I was on the run, not knowing what to think, who to turn to. I checked in daily with the same results from the hospital. I needed a code to speak with her—at least I knew she was okay.

After a few days, I was arrested by the US Marshalls. To be honest, I was kind of happy. I honestly had not gotten any sleep since this tragedy had happened. I needed some rest. The Marshalls took me to the Southern District Police Station which is by where I was raised in Cherry Hill (Baltimore, Maryland).

Some woman detective came in and briefly spoke with me. She mentioned that she knew my mother and she was going to make sure that I was okay. I gave her my lawyer's card. She looked at it and said, "I never heard of him."

She then made copies of my lawyer's card and my driver's license. I was asked random questions by another detective as well. I was then taken to the Baltimore City Booking and intake center, which is pre-trial and where you go to get finger printed, photographed, and officially charged. Upon getting my charge papers, I noticed that I had been charged with multiple accounts of attempted murder and assault. I was lost. I didn't understand. This had to be a mistake. Then I read the statement of the charges: the lady with the Pit bull had lied or assumed I had shot at her. I was being charged for shooting at her. Things just got worse.

I called my mother and father later on that day to tell them what had happened: that I had been arrested, and I was charged for multiple accounts and about the lady with the Pit bull.

This was in September 2019. My life had come to a halt. I had lost so much in a few seconds. I had too many questions. Why did she cheat? Was she okay? Did she lie when she told me she loved me? Did she think about me? One day I broke down crying to my father on the phone. He got quiet and said, "You are strong. Pray. Keep ya head up!"

I said "Okay, Dad."

He then said, "You know a storm is coming, right?"

I said, "Yes, Dad, I'm ready."

He said with a serious voice, "I know you are!"

I replayed that conversation over and over in my head every so often. I thought my father was talking about the storm in my case, but he was talking about a different storm, a storm that I never saw coming, a storm I never was prepared for.

CHAPTER 10

New Generation

Ladders, Drugs, Murder

I was transferred from Baltimore Central Booking and Intake to the pre-trial down in Jessup, Maryland, at Jessup Correctional Institution (JCI). The warden at JCI allowed pre-trial to be housed in two of his buildings (A and B) buildings, due to the limited space that was in Balto City for their pre-trial inmates. To be put plain and simple, it was overcrowded in Baltimore City.

When I arrived at JCI, it was one tier open in A building, and that was B tier, which was supposed to house older guys thirty-five and over. This is where they sent me—B building was open to whomever (old, young, etc.).

Upon getting on B tier in A building, I realize that it was mostly young guys on this tier, eighteen to thirty years old. Many of them moved over here after being whipped, robbed, stabbed, or extorted over B building, and some was just sent over here due to the limited bed space over at B building.

When I got on this tier, I realized two things—number one, prison was not for me anymore, and number two, I was officially an old man. When I tell you I did not know a single soul on this tier—I knew none of these young men.

I had no problem adapting to the environment. One thing for sure is faces may change, but prison doesn't. It's rules to prison among convicts; you live by these rules, you have no problem (mind your business, no ratting, no homosexuality, no talking to COs unless you need toilet paper, medical, or etc.). These are just a few things to remember.

All the young men took to me. Some thought I was younger than what I was due to my youthful looks. I joked with them and said, "No drugs and juices and berries" is why I look so young. We would sit in the day room and talk on the phone, play chess and cards, and talk smack to each other all day long.

The young cats gave me the nickname Uncle Davon. They give guys this name out of a sign of respect, but also when they look at your ass as an old man. LOL!

I use to sit and listen to them beef about who was the best rapper (Money Bag Yo, Durk, Young Boy NBA, L'il Baby, etc.). Damn, I would say "Who are they? What about Pac, Biggie, Nas, Rakim?"

They would look at me like, "Huh? You old as hell, Uncle Davon!" LOL.

I also had to get use to the slang as well—you cappin! "What you mean?" I would ask. That meant someone is lying or faking!

"Yo, you see that ladder when yo ran down on him?"

"Huh? What you talking about ladder?" I would ask. That's an extended clip in a gun.

"Yo, who got OJ, 3, Squares, etc.?"

"Huh? What are y'all talking about?" I would ask.

"Those are drugs, Uncle Davon." Yeah, I was old and lost. LOL.

After being around these young guys, I fell in love with them. Yeah, the slang was different. They loved their rap music and drugs, and it didn't matter if they were Blood, Crip, or BGF, they were just like me—from the hood, real, misunderstood by society, and they just wanted to go home!

I became a tier worker in A building. CO Ms. Bradford hired me. I loved Ms. Bradford; she was a no-nonsense Jamaican woman who would cuss you out one minute and laugh with you the next. I was grateful for the tier man job; it gave me more time out of my cell and longer access to the phone.

One afternoon after I got finished from collecting the trays from feeding lunch to the inmates on the tier, I decided to call Nicole (the blonde bombshell) to see what she was up to. It was a few days after my birthday which was in October. I called Nicole, and the phone rang four times before she answered.

"What's up, woman?" I said to Nicole jokingly.

She was slow to answer. "Hey, Davon!" she said distant like.

"What's wrong with you?" I asked.

She was quiet for a few minutes, then said, "Have you talked to your mother?"

"No, not since my birthday on October 5. Why?"

All Nicole said next was "Bae, call home then call me back."

I knew something was wrong from the way Nicole had sounded. I figured it was something with my little brother because he is always doing something stupid, so I called my mother.

The phone rang one time before my mother answered the phone. When my mother answered, all she said was "Son, son, son!" through her tears. That's all she said. I never heard my mother sound so weak as if she couldn't get her words out, as if someone was choking her and she could barely breathe.

"Ma, what is wrong?" was all I could say.

"He is gone, son—your father is gone!"

Blood rushed to my head, I became light-headed, weak, sad—vulnerable! With tears forming in my eyes, feeling like a scared, in denial child, all I could say was "Who, Father?" Not so, this couldn't be true—not my dad, not King Bomar…nah. My father would and could outlive me; I just talked to him a few days ago on my birthday.

It was true. My father suffered a heart attack on October 7, 2019. Melvin Lee Bomar Jr. was no longer here with me—my backbone. God needed him for greater things in heaven with him. This was the storm my father had mentioned to me a few weeks prior—a storm I was not ready for.

Even though I was in prison, feeling lost, helpless, lonely, a few good men came to me and said, "We are here for you if you need to talk." Carlos from East Baltimore was one of the first. My comrade J Rock made sure the rec hall was quiet the day of my father's funeral, so I could talk over the phone and read a poem that I wrote for my father to everyone that attended his funeral. I want to thank all the men who was down JCI (A building Pre-trial) on October 2019 for being supportive—you all know who you are.

In the midst of my sorrow, I lost faith. Yeah, I know and believe in a higher power, but I read my Bible and pray daily—well at least I try to, so why was God taking me through this? Maybe I'm praying to the wrong god, maybe I'm not praying hard enough. I had no answers, no real shoulder to cry on. My loved one was going through their own problems, so I didn't want to be any more of a burden.

But one day in March 2020, six months after being incarcerated, I got some mail. A smile came across my face, a blessing!

So I thought.

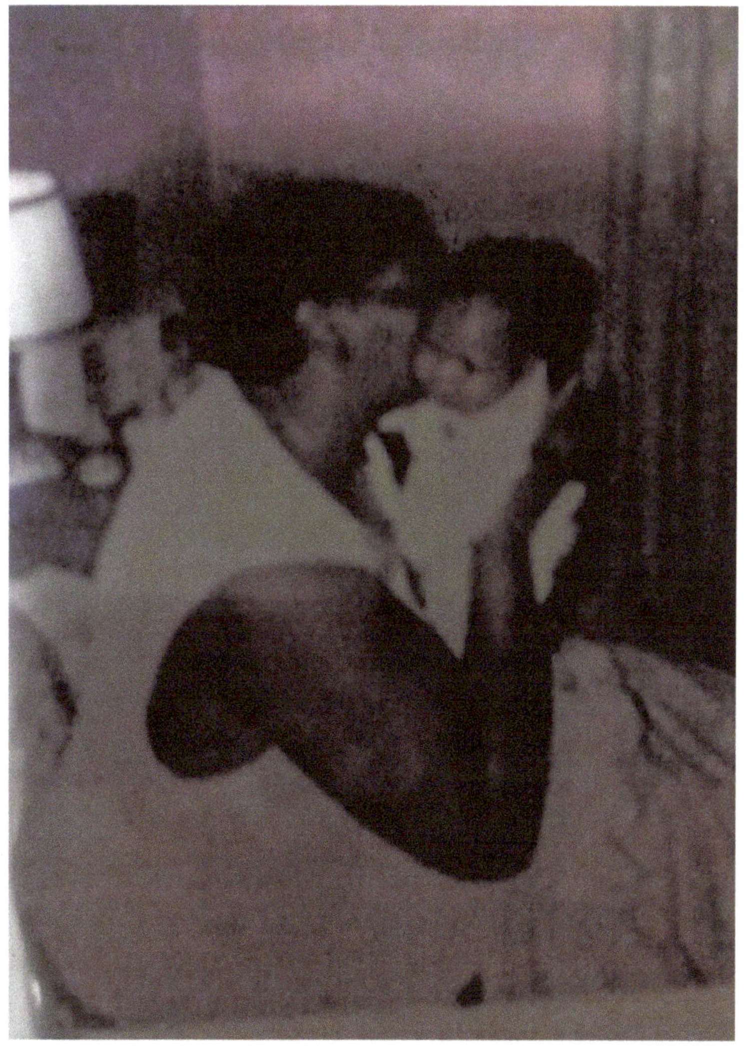

Me and Granny when I was two months old (1975)

My mother (my twin), Dad (my hero), and me:
2017 at the bus station. I just came home.

My father (King Bomar), My li'l brother (Links),
and me at my mother's house in 2017
I love my dad.

Nicole (the blonde bombshell) and me in Philly 2017

Nina (my angel) and me—2019 in Columbia, Maryland.

My father
"Family over everything."
Rest in Heaven
I love you!

Deidre (Ex-wife) and me—2004 at Popular Hill Pre-Release.

CHAPTER 11

The Trial

Lies, Games, Deceit

The CO stopped past my cell. "Roberts, you have mail. What's your ID number?"

"Smith, you know it's me. You just told me I had mail," I said to CO Smith, but I gave him my ID number anyhow.

I looked at the return address to see if I recognize the handwriting or name, but I didn't, so I ripped open the envelope and began to read. By the time I got to the sixth line of the letter, tears filled my eyes—not tears of pain or sorrow, but tears of joy, relief, happiness, love. It was a letter from her, my ex-girlfriend. She was out of the hospital, and she was okay and wanted me to call her. God does hear prayers and answers them.

I called her; we talked daily. That's an understatement—we talked several times a day, all day. We talked about the past. She said she regretted grabbing the gun and know I did not shoot her or at the lady with the Pit bull. She told me how she looked up the reviews on the lady who gave us the lie detector test, and the lady had lied to other people. She told me she still loved me. I told her I love her as well; I was just happy that she was okay.

I talked on the phone from day through night. I no longer played cards or chess. I just wanted to be close to her as possible, and the phone was the only option considering that COVID-19 shut everything down, including our face-to-face visits. We did have Skype visits, and the first time that I'd seen her since that day was so nice. She was so beautiful. We couldn't stop smiling and staring at one another. It felt so good. I was stuck. Again.

A few months had passed, and we was talking on the phone. Things was so good. I no longer cared if the lie detector test was correct or not; I just wanted for us to be happy.

One day she came out the blue and asked me. Was I ready for her? I said yes with no hesitation. I knew what she meant; yes, I was ready to marry her. I got off of the phone and called my best friend, Nina. I trusted Nina to take care of all of my personal business, as well as have access to my savings account.

I called Kay Jewelry store, got some pictures and prices of engagement rings, and had Nina pick it up for me. I was very happy. I proposed to my girlfriend over the phone with Nina taking the ring to her. It was a great day. She said yes; we was engaged. A few months later, the Division of Corrections moved all the pre-trial inmates out of JCI because the warden of JCI needed his housing units for guys in his prison who had time, so on April 2021, we all left Jessup, Maryland, and headed back to Baltimore City. Metropolitan Transition Center (MTC) is where I landed.

Upon arriving at MTC, I honestly thought I wouldn't like being there, considering I would be sleeping in a hundred-man dorm with loudness at hours of the night. Yeah, I had been at MTC before back in 1998 when it was a minimum-security unit for DOC inmates. I had enjoyed it then, but I was twenty-three years younger, and now, being an old man, I didn't mind my peace and quiet behind the close door.

The benefit of being at MTC is we had late nights on the weekend, so phones went off at 2:00 a.m. Plus, I had my COVID-19 vaccination shots which permitted me to have face-to-face visits. I guess MTC isn't too bad after all.

My fiancée and I enjoyed the late-night phone calls and face-to-face visits. Now it was one more hurdle to overcome. It was time to get back home to my family. It was time to go to trial. God was with me, and I was ready.

My trial was July 23, 2021. I have not seen my lawyer the entire time I had him. He came to visit me one time while I was at JCI, which was in June 2020. I asked him numerous times to come and visit me, but he either blamed it on COVID-19 or some later date, which never came.

Now that it was trial time, I had no clue to what strategy we would use because I haven't seen this lawyer in over an entire year. He got my ten thousand dollars and basically put me on the back burner. The day of the trial he advised me of two things: number one, my original judge was switched out with a new judge at the last minute by a no-nonsense judge who once was a top Baltimore County prosecutor (go figure), and number two, the state had made me a last and final offer of eighty-five years all suspended, but twenty-eight years, which he advise that I take—huh? When you got paid that ten thousand dollars last year, you said you fight for wins, not deals. Now this?

I told my lawyer, "Since you feel that way, tell them I would take twenty years."

My lawyer looked me in my eyes and said, "They won't take that, so let's go to trial." Damn, did he even ask him about my counteroffer? I will never know.

My trial lasted five days, from July 23 to 28, 2021. I had many supporters come out every day of my trial (my mother, Nina, Nicole, Hanky, Peedy, Malik, Nell, Dizzy, Hanky's mother, Toya) and a few others. I needed to see those faces and show of love.

The victims got on stand. My fiancée told the jury that I did not shoot her. The prosecutor called her a liar and our engagement a Kay commercial—huh? The second victim (the woman with the Pit bull) told them she never seen me shoot at her, but she heard a bullet pass her ear as she was running away. Huh? Heard a bullet pass your ear—like in the movies? I guess the jury sided with the lady with the Pit bull because she was a young Caucasian woman who portrayed herself as a superhero. Oh yeah…my Jury was made up of nine white jurors, three Black jurors. On day two of the trial, one of the black Jurors could not make it (family matters), so now it was ten white Jurors.

The prosecutor played some video that was not permitted to be played because it was not supposed to be in my motions hearing.

When my lawyer heard the video be played that was not supposed to have been, he asked the judge for a mistrial. She said *no*! Huh?

On the last day of trial I told my lawyer that "I wanted to testify on my own behalf."

He looked at me and said, "I do not think that would be a good idea" because the prosecutors would be able to ask me about my prior convictions.

I told him, "I don't care. This prosecutor is making me sound like a monster with his lies." My lawyer was mad.

He went outside of the courtroom and told my mother to tell me not to get on stand, or I may get life. My mother had a fit when she heard the word "life." She trusted this lawyer when now we realize he didn't mean us no good. I told my mother, "I'm fighting for my life. I'm getting on that stand."

When the prosecutor heard that I was getting on the stand, he asked the judge if we could approach the bench. She said, "Yes." When we got to the bench, the prosecutor told the judge to let Mr. Roberts know (as if I was not at the bench with them) that "If he testifies, I will play a jail call that was recorded of him having phone sex with a young woman who is not his fiancée." Low blow! This taped phone call had nothing to do with the trial or case, but he wanted to embarrass me and the young lady in front of the jury, friends, and my mother on top of assassinating the character of the women and I. Games he played to get a win. I did not testify, and that decision hunts me to this day.

On July 28, 2021, the jury rendered their decision: I was found guilty of two counts of second-degree attempted murder. Sobs, loud cries, tears rolled down my cheeks. My lawyer walked out there with the prosecutor and told him, "Good job!" I was to return on October 5, 2021, to be sentenced.

In the months following my guilty decision, my fiancée and I became kind of distant. She was in a whole other mode, and it was obvious that I was no longer as much a part of it. Arguments were often—any reason not to talk to me as much; I know the deal. Her hopes were on me coming home. Now that I wasn't, there's not much need for me, my opinion, or my love any more—damn… stuck again!

Come to find out that my ex-fiancée was texting one of my so-called friends who gave her his number while at the courthouse during my trial—and I called him my brother.

CHAPTER 12

Sentencing Day

October 5, My B-day—A Day to Always Remember

This was my day—not just my birthday, but the day I was to be sentenced. I left MTC feeling optimistic. I could not sleep at all the night before, but I did not feel tired—nervous, yes, but I kept my poker face on.

I got to the courthouse. Nina had on a "Happy Birthday Davon" shirt on. I saw my mother, Nicole, Dizzy, Hanky's mother, and my ex-fiancée.

My mother, ex-fiancée, and Hanky's mother spoke on my behalf. I said my piece, then I sat down and waited for the judge to speak. The judge sentenced me to eighty years in the Maryland Department of Corrections (thirty years for each count of attempted murder and twenty years for felony use of a firearm to all run consecutive to a total of eighty years).

I took a deep breath to stop from passing out. Just thinking back on it now, I get light-headed.

Upon arriving back to MTC, all the inmates and some of the COs had heard about my sentence already. How? I was on the news—12:00 p.m., every channel.

A few COs felt uncomfortable around me because they said I had too much time to be there and they wanted me out of there. Two COs showed me a lot of love: CO Ms. Carter, whom I had known prior to coming to MTC, and CO Ms. Ellis with the short blonde hair. She would always ask if I was okay.

Sergeant Taylor of Intel would ask me why I was smiling if I had eighty years. I told him, "Because I am blessed, and I will never allow you to see me broken."

So there you have it—eighty years I have, no more fiancée. A few less friends, not much from the outside world anymore. God showed me who really are true, and to the others,

I'm just buried alive.

SHOUT-OUTS

I want to first thank God for giving me the strength to stay positive in the midst of all that the devil throws my way. Without God, I would not have made it this far.

I want to thank Nina. You are my biggest fan and supporter, and you are an angel sent from God. I love you! To my mother (Ms. Boodie), I love you, Ma. Stay strong. I will be back home with you soon enough. To my father (Dad), I miss you. I have your courage to make it through the storm; plus, I have you, Granny, Aunt Dee-Dee, and cousin Shawn watching over me. Y'all, rest in peace. I love y'all.

To Nicole Jones, we are not together anymore, but I thank God for the friend I found in you. I love you! To my brothers (Peedy, Dizzy from Philly, and Malik), thank you for holding me down. To my Cherry Hill family who stopped by to check on my mother, thank you—Cherry Hill for life!

To my comrades, we built George Jackson strong! To all the men and women all over behind the wall, never stop fighting to be free. Stay prayed up!

To CO Ms. Ellis at MTC, I told you I would shout you out. Thank you! To everyone who forgot about me or crossed me, God loves you!

Faith, Toya, Aunt Dot, I love y'all!

To my two sons, Davon and Man-Man, we don't talk as much as a father and son should, and I apologize. I've been so caught up in fighting for my freedom that I neglected you. Forgive me… I love you two so much.

To my niece, Aniyah, I love you. Your photos put a smile on my face. To my stepson James in South Carolina, your conversation helps me a lot. I love you. Thank you!

To Benny Bop, Ruben, Rudy, and Ms. Michelle:
I love y'all. Rest in peace.

To the Cherry Hill crew who is at JCI with me (Conrad, Clayton, Li'l Nell, Scrap Iron, Day-Day, Uncle Rick), we will be back soon. To all men and women behind the wall, *never stop fighting!*

GOD, one more time! I love you!

Coming Soon

Davon Roberts
presents

VA
(Veronica Ave.)
Boyz

About the Author

Davon is a forty-six-year-old from South Baltimore (Cherry Hill). He has two sons, seventeen and twenty-eight years old. He currently has his appeal in to get back in court. To write to him, the address is below.

Davon Roberts #484-170
PO Box 534
Jessup, Maryland 20794

He has his court transcripts for anyone looking to help with his case via PDF, email, or DVD.